How To Get Customers In Your Network Marketing Company

The Complete Guide To Converting Leads To Loyal Customers

By: Argena Olivis

www.networkmarketingkingdom.com

Bonus Video: How To Get Leads and Customers Online

Subscribe To Get Free Tips On How To Generate Leads and Get Customers

When you subscribe to get network marketing tips via email, you will get free access to exclusive subscriber-only resources. All you have to do is enter your email address to the right to get instant access.

These resources will help you get more out of your business – to be able to reach your goals, have more motivation, be at your best, and live the life you've always dreamed of. I'm always adding new resources, which you will be notified of as a subscriber. These will help you get an endless amount of leads and customers.

Visit:

www.networkmarketingkingdom.com/video

to Access The Bonus Video

Table Of Contents

Introduction

Chapter 1: How To Generate Leads

Chapter 2: How To Turn Leads Into Customers

Chapter 3: How To Make Customers Loyal

Chapter 4: Increase Your Sales

Chapter 5: More Lead Generation Strategies

Chapter 6: Get To Work

Conclusion

Introduction

I want to thank and congratulate you for downloading the book, *"How To Get Customers In Your Network Marketing Company: The Complete Guide To Turning Leads Into Loyal Customers"*.

This book contains proven steps and strategies on how to generate leads and turn them into loyal customers.

Finding customers in your network marketing business is crucial for your success.

This is because it provides you with comfort that you can actually sell the product and make a profit.

Once you know how to sell the product, it will be easier for you to train your team.

As network marketers, we need to see a profit right away in order to truly believe in the industry and stay involved in it.

Sales of your product give you that "right now" money. We need that "right now" money to invest in our marketing efforts and promote our opportunity.

In this book, you will learn the following:

- How to generate leads

- Having the right mindset

- How to turn leads into customers

- How to make your customers loyal to you

- How to increase your sales

- More lead generation strategies for both online and offline

As a business owner, you know that it's

necessary to invest in yourself and in your business.

By purchasing this book, you are increasing your value. The more you study and take action, the more results you will see.

So learn how to generate leads and get more customers with these proven marketing strategies.

Thanks again for downloading this book, I hope you enjoy it!

Chapter 1: How To Generate Leads

Get Your Mindset Straight

Before we begin generating leads we need to make sure that you have the right mindset.

Network marketing is not an easy industry. But if you have a product you believe in, you should know in your heart and in your mind that you can be successful.

You have to be able to take rejection as a learning experience. If any of the strategies you take action on don't work for you, tweak them to make them work for you.

Your mindset has to be right. And you have to stay motivated and consistent to win.

Here are some tips on staying motivated daily:

- read for an hour a day (business or personal development books)

- watch YouTube videos on network marketing and motivation

- listen to business and network marketing podcasts

- work out and eat healthily

- have a daily routine and schedule and stay consistent

- set goals and do the work

- make a to-do list every night before bed

- read positive affirmations in the mirror

- create a vision board

- put a note or picture of the lifestyle you want to live on your laptop

Those are just examples of how to stay motivated. Do all that are suggested to you, or just one. But make sure you're not wasting your precious time.

Once your mindset is right, you can start generating leads.

So, have you done some of the suggested

motivators above? I hope so. Now you're ready to move on and start generating leads.

How To Generate Leads

The number one thing you have to remember is that you ALWAYS want to get contact information.

If you don't get a person's contact information, you just lost a lead and a customer.

There are many ways to get a lead's contact information both online and offline without being invasive.

How To Get Leads Offline

To be honest, it's easier to build your customer base offline than online. This is because you're actually meeting people and talking to people.

People like seeing you to get a sense of trust for you.

Without trust, you cannot create a loyal customer base.

There are many strategies you can use to get leads offline:

- Vendor Shows

- Passive Advertising

- Job Fairs

- Flea Markets

- Tailgating

- Partnering With Stores

- Canvassing

- Parties

Vendor Shows

Vendor shows are shows that are created by organizations or individuals. They find vendors in the area and advertise the show to the public.

The vendors are usually private business owners or representatives from direct sales companies.

This is where vendors can set up a table and sell their products.

You can find vendor shows by Googling vendor shows in your area. Type in your city name, vendor shows, the month and the year you're looking to register for.

Make sure you look for shows in advance. Many of these shows get filled very quickly.

Once you get to the vendor show, it's time to collect leads.

You will be collecting leads by doing a giveaway. Giveaways are perfect for getting leads. It also gives you a reason to talk to people walking by your table.

Ask them if they'd like to enter to win.

Make your giveaways very appealing and put a time limit on it. By doing this it makes it seem realer.

For example: Tell them you're auctioning your giveaway off at 2 pm when the vendor show is over.

Ask everyone if they want to enter to win your prize. If it's slow at the show, go around to each vendor and ask him or her if they'd like to enter.

It's great to make friends with other vendors so they can keep you updated with other shows they are doing.

So if you get a vendors contact info, add them on Facebook immediately so you can keep in touch.

Create a survey to collect contact information. The survey should be small enough that you can fold the piece of paper and put it in a basket for the raffle.

Below is an example of a survey that you can copy and paste into a word document and print out. It should print about two per page.

Replace the information in parenthesis so it is relevant to your company.

Are you currently being serviced by a (Your Company) Representative? YES _____ NO___

I would like information about (check all that applies to you):

_____(Your Company) Partner/Helper (collect orders from friends, family, and co-workers,etc.)

_____Purchasing (Your Company) products

_____Receive future (Your Company) brochures

_____(Your Company) Fundraising (school, church, family reunion, other charity)

_____(Your Company) Earning Opportunity (starting my own (Your Company) business)

_____Hosting an Avon Party

THANK YOU for stopping by today

PLEASE PRINT ALL INFORMATION CLEARLY

NAME

_____

ADDRESS_____

—

CITY/STATE/ZIP _____

PHONE _____ **EMAIL**_____

As leads fill this out, fold up the paper and put it in the basket/jar.

If you're just getting to the show, put about three blank ones in there so people will think that a lot of other people find your gift valuable.

People don't like to be the first ones; they like to follow the crowd. It's called "social proof".

Okay, so now you've collected a lot of contact info and you have some idea of what the person is interested in. So when you follow up with them you'll know what to talk to them about.

After the show is over, do your raffle. Most of the leads will have left by now. So just call the winner of your prize on the phone and let them know they won.

Passive Advertising

Passive advertising is another way to get leads, but these are not guaranteed. It's also not as effective as the other strategies. But, it's still worth your time.

Focus your time more on the other strategies, because those are the ones that will get you the most results.

The reason this method doesn't yield many results is because you're not collecting any contact information.

Here are some passive income strategies:

- tear-off fliers

- hanging information on door knobs

- leaving your business cards at the ATM, in library books, and in magazines

- Dropping your books/brochures places

Tear off flyers

Create tear-off flyers with your company's information and your contact information.

If interested, leads will be able to tear off one of the tabs on the flyer in order to take the contact information with them and call you later.

If you want to make the offer more appealing, tear off two of the tabs yourself, this will make people think it's a better offer.

Hanging information on doorknobs

In order to do this, you will need to have some of your company's promotional information such as books or flyers.

Put them in clear promotional bags that you're able to hang on doorknobs.

Go around your neighborhood and hang these on door knobs.

You can also use this method to hang your information other places like bathroom stalls, billboards, and more.

Get creative, the more information you get out there the more leads you'll generate.

Leaving Your Business Cards

Leave your business cards everywhere you go. You never know who's looking for what you have to offer.

Some great places to leave them consistently are: the ATM, in relevant library books, and in relevant magazines.

TIP Staple a sample of your product to your business card and hand it out to everyone. If you have a sample of your product attached you're more likely to get a call if they try the product.

Consistently do this and you will get a few calls. Every call counts. Just think, once you turn that lead into a customer, that can be worth hundreds of dollars in the future.

Dropping

The term "dropping" means you just leave your sales material somewhere for others to find.

This is another passive strategy, but it can still bring you in some leads.

You can drop sales materials in relevant local businesses, on the bus, doctor's offices, office buildings, and other places.

Job Fairs

Job fairs are not just for recruiting, you can also get some sales too. Most people won't want to join your company.

Many people at job fairs are looking for jobs, not to start a business.

But you don't have to lose out.

Collect their contact information by using the survey method outlined in the vendor show section.

Flea Markets

Flea markets are perfect because they are cheap, and the people there love to win free things.

You'll get a lot of leads by using the survey/raffle method outlined in the vendor show section.

Find local flea markets in your area by Googling.

Tailgating

This is a "best kept secret" method that many companies haven't gotten into.

Tailgating is great because you can collect leads right on the spot.

Tailgating is when you open your trunk and set up a "mini vendor show or job fair", and leads will stop by and see what you're giving away.

Create a sign that says "Free (your company's name)". Give out samples to anyone who stops by and asks what's free.

Make sure you're tailgating in an abandoned parking lot or a shopping plaza that you have gotten permission from to do so.

Wherever you decide to tailgate, make sure it's in a busy place with a lot of traffic.

Use the survey/raffle method from the vendor shows section to collect leads.

Partnering with stores

Ask local businesses that are not in competition with your product if you can set up outside their store.

You're most likely to get a yes if you have something of value to offer them. The business is going to want to know what's in it for them.

Here are some ideas you can use to add value to a store when asking if you can set up outside:

- I will recommend your store to my

customers

- I will do an employee appreciation for your workers

- I will do a customer appreciation and give out free samples to all the people that spend a certain amount in your store

- I will put your flyer in all of the promotional material I pass out

- I will not sell anything, I'll just talk about my business opportunity

- I can give you the names and emails of my customers

Once you get the okay to set up a table outside

the business use the survey/raffle method outlined in the vendor show section.

Canvassing

Don't forget about old-fashioned canvassing. Go do-to-door and collect contact information.

You can do this by using the survey/raffle method, or just by simply asking for it and putting it in your phone.

This is the most up close and personal that way that you can get out of all of these results.

It's definitely worth a try. It depends on how bad you want it. Network marketing loves speed, and by canvassing, you will definitely be on the ball with leads.

Tell the lead about your product and how it can benefit them. How can you add value to them?

Make sure to leave them samples and promotional materials.

Let them know you're from their neighborhood and you're only a call away. This will build tons of trust.

Parties

Parties are another way to get leads. Pick a date to have a party, but make sure it's, at least, two weeks in advance.

Send out physical invitations to the people you want to invite. These can be current customers or people you want to become customers.

Next create a Facebook event. If you know someone is active on social media and they have accepted your invite for your Facebook event, there is no need to send them a physical invitation too unless you want to.

Your invitations and Facebook event should have a number that guests can call to RSVP.

***Tip: Put a coupon in the invitation and on the Facebook event. Say if they bring a friend they get a free gift.

Follow up with the guests two days before the event and the day before the event to see if they still plan to attend.

Once you know how many people plan to attend

make sure you have everything set for the party.

Create an agenda of what you want to go over, products you want to introduce, and games you want to play.

Remember to block out sometime in the middle of the party for people to place their orders. This ensures that if someone has to leave early you can still get his or her order.

A typical list of things you'll need for a party:

- order forms

- products to show

- samples

- gifts to give for prizes

- light refreshments

- pens/pencils and paper

- party games

- your agenda

Once you get some confirmed guests set up for your party. Make sure to have a sign-in sheet to collect leads. The sign in sheet should collect information similar to the vendor/raffle survey.

The Takeaway

Generating leads offline is pretty easy, but it's a time commitment. When going out advertising your business work it around your schedule.

Keep in mind that most people are out and about in the early mornings. So plan accordingly.

If you work a regular job, make the best out of your weekends.

Collect contact information whenever you can. Be creative, and invest in your business.

How To Get Leads Online

Getting leads online is a little harder if you don't have any internet marketing experience. But with these basic tips, you can successfully create leads online if you're consistent.

Take some of these tips and create a daily routine that you can use to constantly generate leads.

Blog

Setting up a blog is fairly easy. But marketing it is a little more difficult due to the increasing number of blogs being made every single day.

First you need to decide what you're going to blog about. Your blog should be marketed around the products your company promotes.

For example, if you're in a weight loss company your blog should be centered on something that will provide value such as healthy eating or weight loss.

Your goal is to provide value to your target lead

so they will want to buy from you. But first you have to create trust, and that can take a while.

So find out what you're going to talk about. Make sure the subject of your blog helps people in some way. The best types of blogs are the kinds that teach people how to do something.

Once you've found how you're going to create value and market your product, register for a domain name.

After you buy your domain name, buy hosting. I recommend a service like Bluehost.

Once you have hosting, install Wordpress. After that process, you're good to go.

If creating a blog is foreign to you I suggest searching for tutorials and YouTube videos that will walk you through the process step-by-step.

After you have your blog set up, this is when you should start creating valuable content.

There is a big learning curve to create a lead-generating website, but for now, just do what you know.

Set up a schedule for how often you will blog. Leads will want to hear from you often to create that bond.

Unfortunately, you cannot just put up a blog post and leads start pouring in. You have to market the blog.

This means you need to drive traffic to it from others sources such as social media, guest posting, writing books, building back-links, email marketing, and other methods.

Search Engine Optimization (SEO) is when you

use keywords, which is where leads will be able to use these words and find your content through search engines.

Once you have some traffic it's time to put an email opt-in form on your blog so you can collect leads.

In order to do this, you'll need an email autoresponder like Aweber.

Once you have everything set up and you're creating content that is relevant to the products you sell, you should start getting leads.

Here are the types of posts you should create to get leads to your blog and onto your email list:

- how to posts (teaching leads how to do something relevant to your target market)

- tutorials (how to use the product you're selling)

- new updates regarding your product

- sales and promotions

After reading this section, if you truly want to learn how to generate leads through your blog make sure you study and learn how to get traffic and market your blog properly.

Instagram

Instagram is the newest social media platform that's owned by Facebook. But it's a great place to collect leads.

There are a lot of people from the younger generation using it, and it's growing every day.

In order to post on Instagram, you're going to need a smartphone to download the app. Or you can use a tablet.

You can view your profile through your desktop, but you cannot post that way.

To get leads on Instagram post the following:

- lifestyle pictures

- pictures of new products

- quote pictures

- funny pictures

- notes

- testimonials (before & after)

Post anything that will provide your viewers with entertainment and value. Start by following some people who promote products similar to what you have to offer.

Then follow the people that are following them. If people are following them this means they're interested in your product.

To get more followers and leads make sure to use hashtags. Hashtags are when you use the "#" sign in front of a word.

You want to use these so more people can find

your posts.

Use hashtags relevant to the product you're promoting.

Twitter

To get leads on twitter make sure you're posting regularly and providing value in every post.

Post things like:

- tips

- tutorials

- quotes

- pictures

When following people, use the same techniques as Instagram, such as hashtags to promote your product.

Pinterest

Pinterest is another new social media site but it can still bring in plenty of leads. Pinterest is more of a visual site. So all you'll be posting is pictures.

Create boards that are eye-catching and relevant to your product. Pin all the pictures from both your blog and company website.

You can also use hashtags on Pinterest.

YouTube

YouTube is one of the best ways to get leads online fast. This is because video outdoes all other forms of lead generation.

Creating a valuable video that will help your target market is a great strategy.

Here are some types of YouTube videos you can create:

- tutorials

- product reviews

- giveaways

Optimize your YouTube videos so you'll get maximum exposure.

To increase your conversions make sure to use the proper keywords in the title, description, and tags so you'll rank in Google and in the search engines.

Have fun on your channel and use YouTube to bring traffic to your products.

Promote Your Company Website

We had a lot of talk about creating your own blog but don't forget about the one that your network marketing company provides for you.

There should be a lot of links going out from

your blog to your company website. Use website links to promote specific products so they can buy right from your site.

Always link to your site and promote your site on your business card, social media, and anywhere else you see fit.

eBooks

Create eBooks relevant to your product and target market. In the eBook put an opt-in offer to collect leads.

eBooks are also a great way to promote your blog

or company website.

The content in your eBook should teach your leads how to do something. Once they find value in what you have taught them they will want to become your customers.

Take Away

Use one or more of these strategies when creating leads online. As I've mentioned, generating leads online is harder than offline.

It will take time and patience, but it will work if

you stick to it.

To save yourself time from being in front of the computer all of the time use systems to automate your online efforts.

For social media, use systems like Hootsuite.

You're able to schedule blog posts and YouTube videos to go out in the future.

Use batching to automate this process. Create a lot of content and schedule it for the week.

You can also have emails going out to your leads automatically with your email software.

Remember to focus on your target market. Your target market is whom you will be focusing on selling to.

Set updates in your planner for when you will be writing posts and posting on social media.

Make a daily routine to promote your company's website on different sites. Post in relevant forums to create leads.

In Conclusion

You now have learned how to generate leads
online and offline. Put these strategies into
action and start getting some results.

In the next chapter, we will discuss how to turn
those leads into customers.

Chapter 2: How To Turn Leads Into Customers

Generating leads is great, but that's not where the money is. You get money when you turn your leads into customers.

This is a simple process that will increase your sales and conversions if you take action.

Following Up

You can generate leads all day, but if you don't follow up all your effort was for nothing.

You have to follow up to make the money. That's just the way it works.

Following Up With Leads Offline

When you've done passive prospecting and you've gotten results, you will start getting calls from leads without having to follow up with them.

These leads are automatically customers because if they're calling you, it's so they can place an order.

As far as the raffle/survey from leads that you've gotten from job fairs, vendor shows, etc., you will have to call them and follow up with them.

Call them the next day, tell them how nice it was to meet them and ask them if they'd like a sample.

Don't call and ask for the order right off the bat. You first want to build a rapport.

If your company has an email database where it sends its own emails or has an address book, upload these contacts into that database the same day you get the info or as soon as possible.

Following Up With Leads Online

This won't take a lot of your effort. Use autoresponders to send out promotional and helpful emails.

The system itself will do the conversion. If you're providing enough value, the leads on your email list will become your customers.

Consistency

This is where you start using your planner. Have a follow-up day where you call customers and see if they'd like to order anything. This can be when a new product has launched or when you think they will have run out of the product.

Constantly follow up with leads. Call them as soon as possible. Be polite and professional when making calls.

If you do this over and over again you're bound to convert many of your leads into customers.

Planning

Plan how many leads you will call and when you will call them.

Set goals for how many customers you will get a week. Make the process fun and simple.

Take Away

The key to turning leads into customers is following up.

Follow up with all the leads you collect as soon as possible.

Chapter 3: How To Make Customers Loyal

Getting a customer is not easy and neither is creating a loyal one. But creating loyal customers is what will truly make you rich.

A customer is great, but a customer that orders from you, and only you all the time is priceless.

Customer List

A customer list is a list of people that has purchased something from you that you are going to want to follow up with.

Use this list to keep track of who got your latest brochures/sales material.

Also, use this list to keep track of who ordered when and when you think they'll need a refill/new product.

You'll have access to a printable customer list to keep you organized later.

The point of this list is to keep track and check off names once you've given them your updated sales material.

Also, check off names when you have followed up with a customer about ordering a product.

Customers will be impressed about how you remembered them, and they won't mind your follow up call.

Thank you cards

Send and/or put thank you cards in customer orders.

If a customer orders from you make sure to thank them every single time.

You can send an email, mail a thank you card, or put it in their order.

This simple gesture will win over customers and make them loyal to you. Most network marketers don't think to do this.

**TIP: Thank you cards are even more special when they're handwritten.

Samples

Your customers absolutely love samples. This is also a great way to introduce a new product to your customers to raise your sales.

You shouldn't mind investing in samples for customers that have already spent money with you. This means that you'll be getting your sample investment back time and time again.

Contests

Stir up some fun with your customer base by doing a contest. You can raffle off a product if they spend a certain amount in your store or you could have a customer of the month contest.

It doesn't matter the contest just make it fun and get all your customers involved.

***TIP: A good contest to have is to see what customers can get you the most referrals

Following Up

Make the follow up a pleasant experience for your customers. Mention how you're thankful that they've purchased from you.

Mention what products they've purchased previously, and if you can get them a better deal, then do it.

Know What Your Customer Likes

Be mindful of what your customers like so if the item goes on sale you can let them know.

They will truly appreciate the effort in trying to save them money on their favorite items.

Also, if a product similar to what they like comes

out you'll be able to recommend the product to them.

Monthly Newsletter

Send your entire customer base monthly newsletters. Don't just send one when there's a sale or promotion.

When sending out your monthly newsletters make sure to have a theme around it. You can choose a holiday for that month or just something fun.

Your customer list can be mailed out physically or sent in an email.

What to include in the monthly newsletter:

- customer of the month

- sales and deals

- coupons

- new products that will be launching

- links back to your social media and blog

- product recommendations

- tutorials on how to use products

- new ideas

- etc.

Add things to your newsletter that will make your customer excited to receive it.

Gifts

Everyone loves gifts. Send your customers gifts. These gifts can be digital or physical.

Make the gift presentable and fun. Also, make sure you add a note for why they are receiving the gift.

Appropriate times to send customers gifts:

- samples of new products

- incentive for ordering online

- birthdays and anniversaries

- holidays

- just because (have a random customer receive a gift every month)

Because of your kindness customers will be loyal to you and excited to shop with you again.

Over deliver

No matter what you do, always over deliver. Go way beyond your customer's expectations and they will never buy from anyone else.

Over deliver on everything: your newsletters, your customer service, the content on your blog and social media, absolutely everything!

When a customer is used to your high-quality customer service, they will stick with you, recommend you, and love you.

Chapter 4: Increase Your Sales

Increasing your sales will be super easy once you know how to generate leads and turn those leads into loyal customers.

But here are some ideas that will maximize your results.

Goal Setting

Set sales goals for yourself. Whether you want to make extra income, supplement your income, or fully replace your income, you're going to need goals.

Weekly goals are perfect when it comes to sales. Have weekly goals of how many leads you want, customers you want, and sales you want.

Every commission scale for network marketing companies is different.

Say you get 40% profit on each sale you make and your best selling product is $20. How many $20 products would you have to sell to make the income you want?

Do the math! This is crucial. You have to do the math so you know exactly how much you need to make to reach your goals.

After you do the math for how much you need to sell, you need to subtract any business related expenses.

Your business expenses may be:

- promotional materials (books/brochures/pamphlets)

- samples

- gifts

- vendor shows

- flea markets

- paper for fliers and ink

- business cards

- stamps and stickers

- crafts

- etc.

Whatever you purchased that week that was business related subtract it from the total you earned.

Keeping track of this on a weekly basis will help

you to form a habit of recording and tracking.

It's best to do this in an excel document or an app of some sort.

Once you know how much the average expenses are for each week you can subtract it from your total automatically so you'll know exactly how much you plan to make.

If you really want to get on track, budget your samples and sales materials.

For example: Have a $20/month budget for

samples ($5/wk).

TIPSet a goal for how much you plan to make weekly.

Work Hard

Have you ever heard the saying its called net "work" marketing not net "lazy" marketing?

Well, the saying is true.

Get out there: invest in yourself and your business. Network marketing not only increases your money but it also increases your confidence.

You will find it easier to talk to others, and you will truly grow as a person.

Set up your daily routine for success, and get out there and work your plan.

Get Your Name Out There

You truly have to market your business daily to see success.

Get out there and create partnerships with other

entrepreneurs.

You can truly scale up your business by knowing the right people in the right places.

Someone with more influence can take you to the next level. So always be getting your name out there.

Maximize Finding Leads

Finding leads is an income producing activity.

You should be spending most of your time following up with leads because they can potentially become your customers.

The more leads the better. If you see a shortage of customers, go out a and generate more leads and convert them.

Be The "Go To" Person For Your Product

If someone asks about a specific product, and you're selling it, your name should come to their mind.

The company you are in is already branded, that's what corporate does.

But you have to brand yourself to be the go-to person for your product. When they think of "(insert your product name here)" they should think of you.

Find every single thing you can do to dominate the niche for the product you sell.

You have to get yourself out there. Do video tutorials, product demonstrations, product reviews, and the whole nine.

You have to know your products, and how to use them.

Invest Back Into Your Business

Once you start making more money because of your increased sales, it's time to scale up your business.

Invest back into your business and into yourself.

The more your increase your skills, the more you

will increase your sales.

Invest in more training and materials for your business. You will get your investment back ten times over if you continue to work hard and take action on what you learn.

Chapter 5: More Lead Generation Strategies

Lead generation is going to be what keeps your business going. If you run out of people to talk to, you will get frustrated and quit.

This is why I added more strategies on how to generate leads both online and offline.

Lead Generation Offline

Your offline efforts are just as important as your

online efforts. In the beginning, you should be building your customer base both on and offline for maximum results.

Then once you generate enough customers online and you want to continue to work from home you can convert your offline customers to online customers.

Warm Market

Your warm market is the people you know. Make sure to tap into this market for sales; they will be your main customers.

Call every person in your phone and ask if it'd be

okay if you send him or her a sample or book/brochure/pamphlet. Then follow up with them.

Your warm marketing is where you'll get most of your sales from at first. It's a great place to start but if you want to make money always expand.

Cold Market

Your cold market is going to be a little harder to convince. This is why you need to make sure they're also your target market.

Your target market is the people who are actively searching for your products, solutions to your products, or have a need for your product.

Once you meet these people and get their contact information at vendor shows, flea markets, and job fairs make sure to follow up with them.

Local Chamber of Commerce

Make sure to register at your local chamber of commerce. This is not free but it will get you updates on the local events.

You'll also get to meet lots of other people who can become leads if you get their information.

Community

You should be the go-to person for your product in your community. If there are other people that sell in your community and are not on your team, you should be the one who your neighbors go to.

Totally dominate your community. Market you're business so everyone knows what you do and want to buy from you.

Lead Generation Online

Online is truly what you want to strive for. But in the beginning, don't be too lazy to go offline and do what you have to do.

Message Facebook Friends

Send a message to your Facebook friends who can use your product. Ask them "would it be okay if I give you a sample of "(your product)"?

They will say yes. Make sure you get them some samples A.S.A.P. and follow up with them within two days. Ask how they liked the sample and if you can get them a "book/brochure/pamphlet".

Pay Per Click Ads

Pay per click advertising is another way you can generate leads. This method is mainly used for those who have a bigger budget when starting out.

If your budget allows look into advertising on Google or on Facebook.

Chapter 6: Get To Work

In this book you have learned how to:

- generate leads

- turn leads into customers

- make your customers loyal

- increase your sales

- generate leads online and offline

- stay motivated

Now all you have to do is put what you learn into

action and you will have success if you do.

Reading is great, but it will get you nowhere if you don't apply what you read.

I truly want you to get out there and test these strategies because they do work if you do.

You deserve a business and the financial freedom that comes along with it. If you want it bad enough you will truly implement this information and go to the top!

Now go out there, generate some leads, and

most importantly... follow up. Will you be the next network marketing success story?

Work on your mindset daily and create a daily routine for your business.

We are defined by our habits. Have habits of working smart and hard.

Conclusion

Thank you again for reading *How To Get Customers In Your Network Marketing Company*!

I hope this book was able to help you to get more customers in your network marketing company.

The next step is to go out and generate some leads.

Thank You!

Finally, if you enjoyed this book, then I'd like to ask you for a favor. Would you be kind enough to leave a review for this book on Amazon? It'd be greatly appreciated!

By leaving a review you help other marketers

find the book and it also gives me feedback on the book; your review will let me know what I can improve on or what I've done well.

Thank you and good luck!

Preview Of Network Marketing Mindset: Personal Development and Confidence Building for Network Marketers

Chapter 1: Believe In Yourself and Your Business

Believing in yourself sounds easy, but it's one of the hardest things to do. This is because today there is so much competition and it seems like you'll never get a piece of the pie.

But what you have to realize is, there's always going to be someone better than you at something.

Don't ever waste your time trying to compare yourself to others. It's okay to model them in order to strive for what they have, but it's never okay to compare yourself.

You don't know what it took to achieve what they have. Maybe they have more time than you, maybe they don't have any kids, maybe they work 15 hour days, you just never know.

Don't compare their situation to yours. You also don't know how long they've been doing what they're doing.

When you look at successful network marketers

you don't see the late nights and the studying and skill building it took for them to get to where they are.

They may have poured hundreds and thousands of dollars into their education. You just don't know-- so don't compare.

To believe in yourself you have to learn to stop comparing yourself and start working on yourself.

You can start by asking yourself the most important question: "Is network marketing right for me?":

Network marketing does have a ton of benefits but realize that it's a people business and you have to depend on people in order to make money.

Also, realize you don't have a lot of control of your business, your company can change the compensation plan at any time.

But one thing does remain the same, you can earn as much as you want. There is not a cap. Also, the start cost is low, and you gain confidence by interacting with others.

There are many pros and cons, but are you down for whatever is yet to come? Are you willing to deal with people quitting and your company changing its policies?

If so, you believe in your business and the business model....

Visit
wwww.NetworkMarketingKingdom.com
to check out of Network Marketing Mindset

Or go to: **http://amzn.to/1tHUqD5**

Check Out My Other Books

Below you'll find some of my other popular books that are popular on Amazon and Kindle as well. Simply search the names of the books check them out. Alternatively, you can visit my author page on Amazon to see other work done by me.

<u>Network Marketing Mindset: Personal Development and Confidence Building for Network Marketers</u>

<u>Internet Marketing For Network Marketers: How To Create Automated Systems To Get Recruits and Customers Online</u>

<u>Network Marketing Selling Secrets: 50 Ways To Get New Customers Online and Offline</u>

<u>Network Marketing For Introverts: Guide To Success For The Shy Network Marketer</u>

If the links do not work, for whatever reason, you can simply search for these titles on the Amazon website to find them.

Bonus Video: How To Get Leads and Customers Online

Subscribe To Get Free Tips On How To Generate Leads and Get Customers

When you subscribe to get network marketing tips via email, you will get free access to exclusive subscriber-only resources. All you have to do is enter your email address to the right to get instant access.

These resources will help you get more out of your business – to be able to reach your goals, have more motivation, be at your best, and live the life you've always dreamed of. I'm always adding new resources, which you will be notified of as a subscriber. These will help you get an endless amount of leads and customers.

Visit:

www.networkmarketingkingdom.com/video

to Access The Bonus Video

www.ingramcontent.com/pod-product-compliance
Lightning Source LLC
Chambersburg PA
CBHW070819180526
45168CB00002B/680